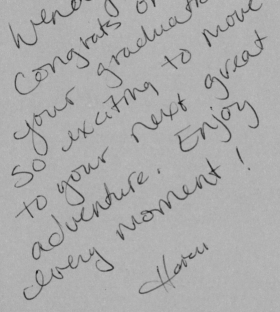

Wendy,
Congrats on
your graduation.
So exciting to move
to your next great
adventure. Enjoy
every moment!

Karen

CONGRATULATIONS
on your
GRADUATION

summersdale

CONGRATULATIONS ON YOUR GRADUATION

An Hachette UK Company
www.hachette.co.uk

Summersdale Publishers Ltd
Part of Octopus Publishing Group Limited
Carmelite House
50 Victoria Embankment
LONDON
EC4Y 0DZ
UK

www.summersdale.com

Printed and bound in China

ISBN: 978-1-78783-525-2

Substantial discounts on bulk quantities of Summersdale books are available to corporations, professional associations and other organizations. For details contact general enquiries: telephone: +44 (0) 1243 771107 or email: enquiries@summersdale.com.

TO Wendy

FROM Heidi

MY DEAR,
TERRIFIED GRADUATES,
YOU ARE ABOUT TO ENTER
THE MOST UNCERTAIN
AND THRILLING PERIOD
OF YOUR LIVES.

LIN-MANUEL MIRANDA

I WAS SMART
ENOUGH TO GO
THROUGH ANY
DOOR THAT
OPENED.

JOAN RIVERS

CAPS OFF TO YOU!

YOUR EDUCATION
IS A DRESS REHEARSAL
FOR A LIFE THAT IS
YOURS TO LEAD.

NORA EPHRON

WHAT WE
LEARN WITH
PLEASURE
WE NEVER
FORGET.

ALFRED MERCIER

STEP INTO THE
NEW STORY YOU
ARE WILLING
TO CREATE.

OPRAH WINFREY

THE ADVENTURE STARTS HERE

DON'T JUST GET
INVOLVED. FIGHT FOR
YOUR SEAT AT THE TABLE.
BETTER YET, FIGHT FOR
A SEAT AT THE HEAD
OF THE TABLE.

BARACK OBAMA

SUCCESS IS NEVER FINAL. FAILURE IS NEVER FATAL. IT'S COURAGE THAT COUNTS.

ANONYMOUS

YOU
DID IT!

THERE ARE
FAR, FAR BETTER
THINGS AHEAD
THAN ANY WE
LEAVE BEHIND.

C. S. LEWIS

YOUR LIFE IS YOUR STORY, AND THE ADVENTURE AHEAD OF YOU IS THE JOURNEY TO FULFIL YOUR OWN PURPOSE AND POTENTIAL.

KERRY WASHINGTON

CHAMPIONS
ARE MADE FROM
SOMETHING THEY HAVE
DEEP INSIDE THEM —
A DESIRE, A DREAM,
A VISION.

MUHAMMAD ALI

BOUNCE BACK
FROM EVERY "NO"
AND YOU'LL FIND
THE BEST "YES"

THERE IS NO SCRIPT. LIVE YOUR LIFE. SOAK IT ALL IN.

DICK COSTOLO

IF YOU'RE NOT MAKING SOME NOTABLE MISTAKES ALONG THE WAY, YOU'RE CERTAINLY NOT TAKING ENOUGH BUSINESS AND CAREER CHANCES.

SALLIE KRAWCHECK

Dare to
DREAM BIG

THE OLD RULES
ARE CRUMBLING AND
NOBODY KNOWS WHAT
THE NEW RULES ARE.
SO MAKE UP YOUR
OWN RULES.

NEIL GAIMAN

THERE IS
NO WAY TO
SHORT-CIRCUIT
THE PATH TO
SUCCESS.

TORY BURCH

THE WORLD
OF THE FUTURE
IS IN OUR MAKING.
TOMORROW
IS NOW.

ELEANOR ROOSEVELT

EDUCATION IS
ONE OF THE BLESSINGS
OF LIFE — AND ONE
OF ITS NECESSITIES.

MALALA YOUSAFZAI

AN INVESTMENT
IN KNOWLEDGE
PAYS THE BEST
INTEREST.

BENJAMIN FRANKLIN

EVERY ACHIEVEMENT STARTS WITH THE MOTIVATION TO BEGIN

I USED TO WANT
THE WORDS "SHE TRIED"
ON MY TOMBSTONE.
NOW I WANT
"SHE DID IT".

KATHERINE DUNHAM

I CHOOSE TO MAKE
THE REST OF MY LIFE
THE BEST OF MY LIFE.

LOUISE HAY

GIVE IT YOUR ALL.
DARE TO BE ALL
YOU CAN BE.

HILLARY CLINTON

THE WORLD IS YOUR OYSTER

DON'T LET THE NOISE
OF OTHERS' OPINIONS
DROWN OUT YOUR OWN
INNER VOICE... HAVE THE
COURAGE TO FOLLOW YOUR
HEART AND INTUITION.

STEVE JOBS

IF YOU
DON'T RISK
ANYTHING,
YOU RISK
EVEN MORE.

ERICA JONG

DON'T LOOK BACK —
YOU AREN'T GOING
THAT WAY

SUCCESS USUALLY
COMES TO THOSE
WHO ARE TOO BUSY
TO BE LOOKING
FOR IT.

HENRY DAVID THOREAU

START WHERE
YOU ARE. USE
WHAT YOU HAVE.
DO WHAT
YOU CAN.

ARTHUR ASHE

DON'T BE
AFRAID OF FEAR.
BECAUSE IT SHARPENS
YOU, IT CHALLENGES
YOU, IT MAKES
YOU STRONGER.

ED HELMS

Anything

IS POSSIBLE

THE HIGHEST
RESULT OF
EDUCATION IS
TOLERANCE.

HELEN KELLER

EDUCATION IS OUR
PASSPORT TO THE FUTURE,
FOR TOMORROW BELONGS
TO THE PEOPLE WHO
PREPARE FOR IT TODAY.

MALCOLM X

THE ROAD LESS
TRAVELLED IS SOMETIMES
FRAUGHT WITH BARRICADES,
BUMPS, AND UNCHARTED TERRAIN.
BUT IT IS ON THAT ROAD
WHERE YOUR CHARACTER
IS TRULY TESTED.

KATIE COURIC

SELF-TRUST IS
THE FIRST SECRET
OF SUCCESS.

RALPH WALDO EMERSON

TRY NOT TO BECOME
A MAN OF SUCCESS,
BUT RATHER BECOME
A MAN OF VALUE.

ALBERT EINSTEIN

YOU'RE ONE
STEP CLOSER
TO FINDING OUT
WHO YOU'RE
GOING TO BE

GO INTO THE
WORLD AND DO
WELL. BUT MORE
IMPORTANTLY, GO
INTO THE WORLD
AND DO GOOD.

MINOR MYERS JR

NOW THAT YOU'VE
GRADUATED, JUST
REMEMBER: BOSSES
DON'T USUALLY
ACCEPT NOTES FROM
YOUR MOTHER.

MELANIE WHITE

YOU
CAN AND YOU
WILL

IF YOU DON'T
LIKE THE ROAD
YOU'RE WALKING,
START PAVING
ANOTHER ONE.

DOLLY PARTON

GRADUATION IS A
PROCESS THAT GOES
ON UNTIL THE LAST
DAY OF YOUR LIFE.
IF YOU CAN GRASP
THAT, YOU'LL MAKE
A DIFFERENCE.

ARIE PENCOVICI

THE ESSENCE OF KNOWLEDGE IS, HAVING IT, TO APPLY IT. NOT HAVING IT, TO CONFESS YOUR IGNORANCE.

CONFUCIUS

SEIZE THE DAY,
EVERY DAY, AND YOU
WILL SEIZE YOUR
DREAMS

I'M NOT TELLING YOU
IT'S GOING TO BE EASY.
I'M TELLING YOU IT'S
GOING TO BE WORTH IT.

ART WILLIAMS JR

YOU CAN NEVER
LEAVE FOOTPRINTS
THAT LAST IF YOU
ARE ALWAYS WALKING
ON TIPTOE.

LEYMAH GBOWEE

Con-grad
-ULATIONS!

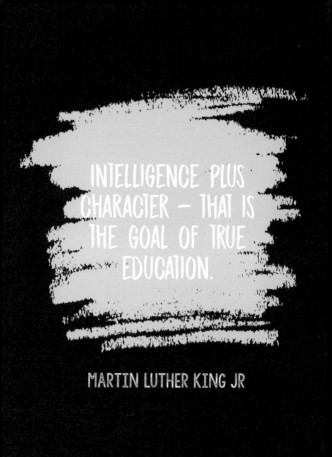

INTELLIGENCE PLUS CHARACTER — THAT IS THE GOAL OF TRUE EDUCATION.

MARTIN LUTHER KING JR

ACCEPT
RESPONSIBILITY
FOR YOUR LIFE. KNOW
THAT IT IS YOU WHO
WILL GET YOU WHERE
YOU WANT TO GO,
NO ONE ELSE.

LES BROWN

A DREAM
DOES NOT
BECOME REALITY
THROUGH MAGIC.
IT TAKES SWEAT,
DETERMINATION
AND HARD
WORK.

COLIN POWELL

THE MERE FACT OF
BEING ABLE TO CALL
YOUR JOB YOUR
PASSION IS SUCCESS
IN MY EYES.

ALICIA VIKANDER

DOUBT KILLS
MORE DREAMS
THAN FAILURE
EVER WILL.

SUZY KASSEM

GOOD THINGS
COME TO THOSE
WHO WORK
FOR THEM!

AT COMMENCEMENT
YOU WEAR YOUR SQUARE-
SHAPED MORTAR BOARDS.
MY HOPE IS THAT FROM
TIME TO TIME YOU WILL
LET YOUR MINDS BE
BOLD, AND WEAR
SOMBREROS.

PAUL FREUND

THE FIRST
OF MANY
GRADUATIONS
IN LIFE. EACH
ONE HOLDS
SUCCESSES FOR
YOU TO ENJOY.

CATHERINE PULSIFER

THERE ARE MANY
THINGS THAT SEEM
IMPOSSIBLE ONLY SO
LONG AS ONE DOES NOT
ATTEMPT THEM.

ANDRÉ GIDE

YOUR EDUCATION
IS SOMETHING YOU
CAN NEVER LOSE

WINNERS TAKE TIME
TO RELISH THEIR WORK...
SCALING THE MOUNTAIN IS
WHAT MAKES THE VIEW FROM
THE TOP SO EXHILARATING.

DENIS WAITLEY

DO NOT WAIT
TO STRIKE TILL THE
IRON IS HOT; BUT
MAKE IT HOT
BY STRIKING.

BENJAMIN FRANKLIN

DEFINE
SUCCESS FOR
YOURSELF

ONCE IN A RARE WHILE,
SOMEBODY COMES ALONG
WHO DOESN'T JUST RAISE
THE BAR, THEY CREATE AN
ENTIRELY NEW STANDARD
OF MEASUREMENT.

DICK COSTOLO

TO
ACCOMPLISH
GREAT THINGS,
WE MUST NOT
ONLY ACT, BUT
ALSO DREAM, NOT
ONLY PLAN, BUT
ALSO BELIEVE.

ANATOLE FRANCE

LIFE SHRINKS

OR EXPANDS IN

PROPORTION TO

ONE'S COURAGE.

ANAÏS NIN

RESULTS HAPPEN OVER TIME, NOT OVERNIGHT. WORK HARD, STAY CONSISTENT, AND BE PATIENT.

ANONYMOUS

FIGHT FOR WHAT
MAKES YOU OPTIMISTIC
ABOUT THE WORLD.
FIND IT, INSIST ON
IT, DIG INTO IT,
GO AFTER IT.

JENNIFER GARNER

YOU CAN'T
CLIMB THE
LADDER OF
SUCCESS WITH
YOUR HANDS
IN YOUR
POCKETS.

ARNOLD SCHWARZENEGGER

THE MORE THAT
YOU READ, THE MORE
THINGS YOU WILL KNOW.
THE MORE THAT YOU
LEARN, THE MORE
PLACES YOU'LL GO.

DR SEUSS

DO NOT FOLLOW WHERE THE
PATH MAY LEAD. GO INSTEAD
WHERE THERE IS NO PATH
AND LEAVE A TRAIL.

RALPH WALDO EMERSON

UNLEASH YOUR
POTENTIAL

THERE ARE NO
REGRETS IN LIFE.
JUST LESSONS.

JENNIFER ANISTON

YOU CANNOT DREAM OF
BECOMING SOMETHING YOU
DO NOT KNOW ABOUT.
YOU HAVE TO LEARN TO
DREAM BIG. EDUCATION
EXPOSES US TO WHAT
THE WORLD HAS
TO OFFER.

SONIA SOTOMAYOR

THE HARDER
THE BATTLE,
THE SWEETER
THE VICTORY

TO TRAVEL
HOPEFULLY IS A
BETTER THING
THAN TO ARRIVE,
AND THE TRUE
SUCCESS IS TO
LABOUR.

ROBERT LOUIS STEVENSON

THE FUTURE CANNOT BE PREDICTED, BUT FUTURES CAN BE INVENTED.

DENNIS GABOR

KNOWLEDGE
IS NOT POWER.
IT IS THE
IMPLEMENTATION
OF KNOWLEDGE
THAT IS POWER.

LARRY WINGET

WHEN YOU
BECOME FEARLESS,
LIFE BECOMES
LIMITLESS

DON'T EVER
UNDERESTIMATE THE
IMPORTANCE YOU CAN HAVE,
BECAUSE HISTORY HAS SHOWN
US THAT COURAGE CAN BE
CONTAGIOUS AND HOPE
CAN TAKE ON A LIFE
OF ITS OWN.

MICHELLE OBAMA

BE THE
HARDEST
WORKING PERSON
YOU KNOW.
BECAUSE IF YOU'RE
NOT, SOMEONE
ELSE WILL BE.

IAN BRENNAN

Be a
TRAILBLAZER

YOU WILL STUMBLE
AND FALL; YOU WILL
EXPERIENCE BOTH DISASTER
AND TRIUMPH, SOMETIMES
IN THE SAME DAY.
BUT... NEITHER TRIUMPHS
NOR DISASTERS
LAST FOREVER.

HELEN MIRREN

I AM A GREAT
BELIEVER IN LUCK.
THE HARDER I WORK,
THE MORE OF IT I
SEEM TO HAVE.

COLEMAN COX

EDUCATION IS THE KEY TO UNLOCKING THE WORLD, A PASSPORT TO FREEDOM.

OPRAH WINFREY

BELIEVING IN
YOURSELF IS THE
FIRST NECESSARY STEP
TO COMING EVEN CLOSE
TO ACHIEVING YOUR
POTENTIAL.

SHERYL SANDBERG

EDUCATION IS THE MOST POWERFUL WEAPON WE CAN USE TO CHANGE THE WORLD.

NELSON MANDELA

YOUR HARD
WORK HAS
PAID OFF!

YOU CAN'T PUT A
LIMIT ON ANYTHING.
THE MORE YOU DREAM,
THE FARTHER YOU GET.

MICHAEL PHELPS

IT'S ALWAYS
A GOOD MOVE TO
LISTEN TO THAT
INNER VOICE...
IF IT DOESN'T LEAD
TO A CRIME.

LISA KUDROW

WHEREVER
YOU GO,
GO WITH
ALL YOUR
HEART.

CONFUCIUS

THE FORMULA OF
HAPPINESS AND SUCCESS
IS JUST BEING ACTUALLY
YOURSELF, IN THE MOST
VIVID POSSIBLE WAY
YOU CAN.

MERYL STREEP

ENJOY THE PROCESS OF
YOUR SEARCH WITHOUT
SUCCUMBING TO THE PRESSURE
OF THE RESULT. TRUST YOUR
GUT. KEEP THROWING DARTS
AT THE DARTBOARD.

WILL FERRELL

TAKE PRIDE IN HOW FAR YOU HAVE COME. HAVE FAITH IN HOW FAR YOU CAN GO.

THE FUTURE

BELONGS TO

THOSE WHO

WORK HARD

DREAMS CAN CHANGE.
IF WE'D ALL STUCK WITH
OUR FIRST DREAM, THE WORLD
WOULD BE OVERRUN WITH
COWBOYS AND PRINCESSES.

STEPHEN COLBERT

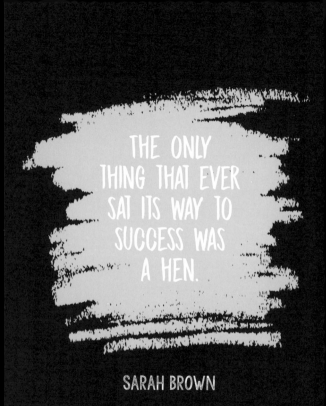

THE ONLY
THING THAT EVER
SAT ITS WAY TO
SUCCESS WAS
A HEN.

SARAH BROWN

SUCCESS IS NOT
THE KEY TO HAPPINESS.
HAPPINESS IS THE KEY
TO SUCCESS. IF YOU LOVE
WHAT YOU ARE DOING,
YOU WILL BE SUCCESSFUL.

ALBERT SCHWEITZER

IF YOU CAN
FIND A PATH WITH
NO OBSTACLES, IT
PROBABLY DOESN'T
LEAD ANYWHERE.

FRANK A. CLARK

WHEN THE WHOLE WORLD IS SILENT, EVEN ONE VOICE BECOMES POWERFUL.

MALALA YOUSAFZAI

THE BEST IS YET TO COME

EVEN IF
YOU ARE ON
THE RIGHT TRACK,
YOU WILL GET RUN
OVER IF YOU JUST
SIT THERE.

WILL ROGERS

TOMORROW'S ILLITERATE WILL NOT BE THE MAN WHO CAN'T READ; HE WILL BE THE MAN WHO HAS NOT LEARNED HOW TO LEARN.

HERBERT GERJUOY

THE MIND
IS NOT A VESSEL
TO BE FILLED,
BUT A FIRE TO
BE KINDLED.

PLUTARCH

DON'T LET
PEOPLE WHO
THINK TOO SMALL
TELL YOU YOUR
DREAMS ARE
TOO BIG

YOU DON'T GO TO
UNIVERSITY SO YOU CAN
PUNCH A CLOCK. YOU GO TO
UNIVERSITY SO YOU CAN BE
IN A POSITION TO MAKE
A DIFFERENCE.

JANET NAPOLITANO

IF WE ALL DID THE
THINGS THAT WE ARE
CAPABLE OF DOING,
WE WOULD LITERALLY
ASTOUND OURSELVES.

THOMAS EDISON

IF YOU LOSE
FOCUS, GET
GLASSES

POWER'S NOT
GIVEN TO YOU.
YOU HAVE TO
TAKE IT.

BEYONCÉ

LEARNING IS
NOT THE PRODUCT OF
TEACHING. LEARNING IS
THE PRODUCT OF THE
ACTIVITY OF LEARNERS.

JOHN HOLT

I HAVE
NEVER LET
MY SCHOOLING
INTERFERE
WITH MY
EDUCATION.

MARK TWAIN

TODAY IS JUST THE
FIRST OF SO MANY
ACHIEVEMENTS

THE CHALLENGE IS
NOT TO BE PERFECT...
IT'S TO BE WHOLE.

JANE FONDA

BE BRAVE.
TAKE RISKS.
NOTHING CAN
SUBSTITUTE
EXPERIENCE.

PAUL COELHO

You
SMASHED IT!

THERE MAY BE DAYS
WHEN YOU'LL SAY TO
YOURSELF, "I CAN'T.
I LITERALLY CAN'T EVEN."
BUT YOU CAN!
YOU CAN EVEN!

KATIE COURIC

NOT ONLY
CAN YOU NOT
PLAN THE IMPACT
YOU'RE GOING TO
HAVE, YOU OFTEN
WON'T RECOGNIZE
IT WHEN YOU'RE
HAVING IT.

DICK COSTOLO

PEOPLE BECOME REALLY
QUITE REMARKABLE
WHEN THEY START
THINKING THAT THEY
CAN DO THINGS.

NORMAN VINCENT PEALE

NEVER LET THE FEAR
OF STRIKING OUT KEEP YOU
FROM PLAYING THE GAME.

BABE RUTH

YOU NEVER SHOULD
SPEND YOUR TIME
BEING THE FORMER
ANYTHING.

CONDOLEEZZA RICE

MAY THE
FRIENDS YOU
MADE LAST
LONGER THAN
YOUR STUDENT
DEBT

YOU CAN FAIL AT
WHAT YOU DON'T WANT,
SO YOU MIGHT AS WELL
TAKE A CHANCE ON DOING
WHAT YOU LOVE.

JIM CARREY

AND WILL
YOU SUCCEED?
YES! YOU WILL,
INDEED! (98 AND
¾ PER CENT
GUARANTEED.)

DR SEUSS

WHO QUESTIONS
MUCH, SHALL LEARN
MUCH, AND RETAIN
MUCH.

FRANCIS BACON

IF YOU GET LOST ON
YOUR WAY TO YOUR
DREAMS, FIND A
BETTER PATH

YOUR TIME
IS LIMITED, SO
DON'T WASTE IT
LIVING SOMEONE
ELSE'S LIFE.

STEVE JOBS

YOU CAN NEVER
BE OVERDRESSED
OR OVEREDUCATED.

OSCAR WILDE

NEVER
STOP PURSUING
KNOWLEDGE

THE
DIRECTION
IN WHICH
EDUCATION
STARTS A MAN
WILL DETERMINE
HIS FUTURE
LIFE.

PLATO

IF YOU HEAR A
VOICE WITHIN YOU SAY
"YOU CANNOT PAINT",
THEN BY ALL MEANS
PAINT AND THAT VOICE
WILL BE SILENCED.

VINCENT van GOGH

EDUCATION'S
PURPOSE IS TO REPLACE
AN EMPTY MIND WITH
AN OPEN ONE.

MALCOLM FORBES

Totally

GRAD-ICAL

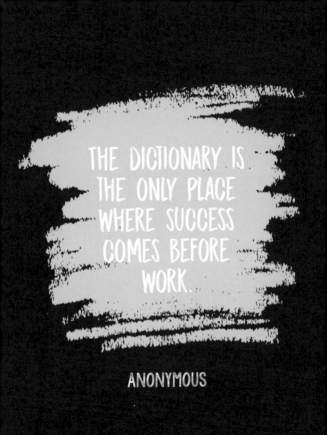

THE DICTIONARY IS THE ONLY PLACE WHERE SUCCESS COMES BEFORE WORK.

ANONYMOUS

THE ONLY THING
YOU CAN DO IN THIS
LIFE IS PURSUE YOUR
PASSIONS, CELEBRATE
YOUR BLOOPERS AND
NEVER STOP FOLLOWING
YOUR FEAR.

GRACE HELBIG

I ENCOURAGE YOU TO LIVE WITH LIFE. BE COURAGEOUS, ADVENTUROUS. GIVE US A TOMORROW, MORE THAN WE DESERVE.

MAYA ANGELOU

DEVELOP A PASSION
FOR LEARNING. IF YOU
DO, YOU WILL NEVER
CEASE TO GROW.

ANTHONY J. D'ANGELO

WITHOUT
LABOUR, NOTHING
PROSPERS.

SOPHOCLES

THE
BEST THINGS
COME TO THOSE
WHO DON'T
GIVE UP

LIFE IS TEN
PER CENT WHAT
HAPPENS TO YOU
AND NINETY PER
CENT HOW YOU
RESPOND TO IT.

CHARLES SWINDOLL

SURE I AM
OF THIS, THAT
YOU HAVE ONLY
TO ENDURE TO
CONQUER.

WINSTON CHURCHILL

MAKE THE MOST
OF YOURSELF BY FANNING
THE TINY, INNER SPARKS
OF POSSIBILITY INTO
FLAMES OF ACHIEVEMENT.

GOLDA MEIR

LET
THE ADVENTURE
BEGIN

LIFE IS MY
COLLEGE. MAY I
GRADUATE WELL,
AND EARN SOME
HONOURS!

LOUISA MAY ALCOTT

TAKE CRITICISM
SERIOUSLY, BUT NOT
PERSONALLY. IF THERE
IS TRUTH OR MERIT
IN THE CRITICISM,
TRY TO LEARN FROM IT.
OTHERWISE, LET IT
ROLL RIGHT OFF YOU.

HILLARY CLINTON

WHEN YOU LEAVE
HERE, DON'T FORGET
WHY YOU CAME.

ADLAI STEVENSON II

If you're interested in finding out more about our books,
find us on FACEBOOK at SUMMERSDALE PUBLISHERS and
follow us on TWITTER AT @SUMMERSDALE.

WWW.SUMMERSDALE.COM